NEW YORK TO CHARLES LINDBERGH DID IT FIRST!

BIOGRAPHY OF FAMOUS PEOPLE

Children's Biography Books

BABY PROFESSOR
EDUCATION KIDS

Speedy Publishing LLC
40 E. Main St. #1156
Newark, DE 19711
www.speedypublishing.com

Charles Lindbergh was one of the most famous Americans in the middle of the twentieth century. What did he do? Let's find out.

The Spirit of St. Louis at the National Air and Space Museum in Washington D.C.

EARLY DAYS

Charles Lindbergh was born in Detroit, Michigan in 1902. His father was a lawyer and a member of the U.S. Congress. He grew up in Minnesota on a farm, and showed a gift with machines and mechanical systems from when he was very young.

Charles with his father Charles Lindbergh Sr.

Charles Lindbergh

He also was fascinated by flying, which was in its early stages (the Wright brothers had flown their plane for the first time in 1903).

He went to college to study to be an engineer. But after just two years he quit college to become a pilot. Lindbergh worked as a *"barnstormer":* he would perform amazing acrobatic stunts in his airplane at fairs and exhibitions.

He sometimes walked out on the wing of the plane he was flying! He was so good, and survived so many scary stunts, that he got the nickname "Lucky Lindy".

In 1924, Lindbergh joined the U.S. Army and got advanced training as a pilot. He graduated from the course number one in his class.

Charles Lindberg as a young officer in the US Army

After his military service, Lindbergh worked as a commercial pilot, flying the mail plane from St. Louis to Chicago and back. He gained experience in all the surprising things that can happen to a small plane and its pilot, from mechanical problems to challenging weather.

The first flight of the Wright brothers aircraft "Wright Flyer I," December 17, 1903. The Wright brothers played a heavy influence on Charles's interest in flying.

SOLO:
NEW YORK TO PARIS

In 1919 a hotel owner offered a prize for the first person who could fly, alone and non-stop, from London to Paris. That very year two Englishmen flew non-stop from Newfoundland to Ireland, where they crashed. But this did not match the terms of the prize.

Col. Charles Lindbergh

Many pilots tried to win the Orteig prize, but none succeeded. Several pilots died in the attempt: it was an incredible challenge both for the solo pilot and for the technology of the planes of that era.

Charles Lindbergh standing beside the Spirit of St. Louis

In 1927 the prize was still waiting. Lindbergh decided to try for it. He found a group of businessmen in St. Louis who would put up the money for a custom-built plane, which Lindbergh helped design.

Lindbergh taking off from the Roosevelt Field

When the plane, named "The Spirit of St. Louis", was ready, Lindbergh did a test run, flying from San Diego to St. Louis and then on to New York City.

Lindbergh took off from New York just before 8 a.m. on May 20. He flew over 3,600 miles in just over 33 hours, landing at Paris on May 21 around 10:30 p.m., local time.

Charles Lindbergh working on the engine of "The Spirit of St Louis."

During the flight, Lindbergh spent a lot of time in fog. He had no landmarks and nothing to look at to keep him alert, so his biggest problem was staying awake. By the time the preparations and the flight itself were done, he had had no sleep for over 55 hours.

Charles Lindbergh c. 1927

At one point he dipped down near the surface of the ocean and opened the cockpit window in hopes that some of the spray off the waves would wake him up a bit. He had hallucinations of mysterious forms flying along with him— and some of them tried to speak to him!

Charles Lindbergh

Lindbergh fought off the hallucinations just before arriving at Paris, and landed in front of a crowd of over 150,000 people.

Fred E. Weick head of NACA Propeller Research Tunnel section, in rear cockpit of Lockheed Sirius (NR211). Charles Lindbergh in front. Tom Hamilton is standing.

NATIONAL HERO

People around the world called Charles Lindbergh a hero. U.S. President Calvin Coolidge gave Lindbergh two medals normally reserved for military success. When he got back to the United States, he was treated to more medals, more awards, and ticker-tape parades. To the nickname "Lucky Lindy" people added a new one: "The Lone Eagle".

Lindbergh spent seven months flying to cities in every state in the United States. He gave speeches to promote interest in flight, and even space flight! He helped Professor Robert Goddard of Clark University in Massachusetts get funding for his experiments that helped develop the rocket ships that would eventually launch satellites, and then people, into space.

Charles Lindbergh delivering the mail from St. Louis to Chicago, flying the mail plane.

After the tour, Lindbergh estimated that he had given 147 speeches in 92 cities, and had traveled almost 1300 miles in parades in his honor. People

Charles and Anne Lindbergh on a flight to China.

became excited about the potential of air travel—even the use of airmail letters, which cost more but went faster than the regular mail, jumped dramatically.

Charles and Anne with the "Sirius" airplane in Japan during their 1931 Orient flight.

At the end of 1927 Lindbergh flew to Mexico and several Central American countries on a good-will mission for the United States. In Mexico he met Anne Morrow, the daughter of the United States ambassador. They eventually married and she joined him on many of his travels in the following years as his co-pilot.

Charles and wife Anne

Anne Morrow Lindbergh in cockpit

Anne Morrow Lindbergh became famous in her own right as a poet and non-fiction writer. Her most popular book was *The Gift from the Sea,* an inspirational book about American women.

INVENTIONS AND CAUSES

Flying was not Charles Lindbergh's only interest. In the early 1930s, he worked with a French surgeon to develop an artificial heart. Others built on this device over the years to help patients who needed heart surgery and similar operations.

Standing in front of a rocket launch tower on Sept. 23, 1935, are (left to right): Albert Kisk, machinist; Harry F. Guggenheim; Dr. Robert H. Goddard; Col. Charles A. Lindbergh and N.T. Ljungquist, machinist. Charles Lindbergh, an advocate for Goddard and his research, helped secure a grant from the Daniel and Florence Guggenheim Foundation in 1930.

Goddard with supporters in New Mexico, 1935. (left to right) Assistant Albert Kisk, financier Harry Guggenheim, Goddard, Charles Lindbergh and assistants Nils Ljungquist and Charles Mansur. (U.S. Air Force photo)

On another front, Lindbergh was a passionate conservationist, saying that in his travels he had become aware of how human activity was putting the Earth in danger. He raised awareness about endangered species, and helped encourage people to donate to conservation efforts. He helped buy the land that became Haleakala National Park in Hawaii.

Lindbergh and Robert Goddard continued their shared work to support the development of space travel. They both had a vision of humans traveling to the moon. In 1968, after the Apollo 8 spacecraft's crew became the first humans to orbit the moon, Lindbergh told the astronauts that they had turned the dream of Robert Goddard into reality.

Astronaut Wally Schirra (sitting 3rd from left), signing a commemorative document, with his Apollo 8 crew, Charles Lindbergh, First Lady Bird Johnson, President Johnson, NASA Administrator Webb and Vice President Humphrey in witnessing.

SORROW

Charles and Anne Lindbergh had a son, Charles Junior. In 1932, when the baby was less than two years old, someone kidnapped him from the Lindbergh home in New Jersey. The body was found about three months later, not far from the house. A man was arrested in 1932, tried, and found guilty of the kidnapping; he was executed in 1934.

Anne Morrow Lindbergh (right), with her mother (rear) and grandmother (center), and son Charles A. Lindbergh, Jr.

To escape the publicity surrounding this sad event, the Lindberghs moved to Europe in 1935. They were hoping for some privacy and a chance to rebuild their lives.

Charles A. Lindbergh testifying before a grand jury, telling his story of the ransom he paid for his son's safe return.

WANTED

INFORMATION AS TO THE WHEREABOUTS OF

CHAS. A. LINDBERGH, Jr.

OF HOPEWELL, N. J.

SON OF COL. CHAS. A. LINDBERGH

World-Famous Aviator

This child was kidnaped from his home in Hopewell, N. J., between 8 and 10 p. m. on Tuesday, March 1, 1932.

DESCRIPTION:

Age, 20 months   Hair, blond, curly
Weight, 27 to 30 lbs.   Eyes, dark blue
Height, 29 inches   Complexion, light
Deep dimple in center of chin
Dressed in one-piece coverall night suit

ADDRESS ALL COMMUNICATIONS TO
COL. H. N. SCHWARZKOPF, TRENTON, N. J., or
COL. CHAS. A. LINDBERGH, HOPEWELL, N. J.

ALL COMMUNICATIONS WILL BE TREATED IN CONFIDENCE

March 11, 1932

COL. H. NORMAN SCHWARZKOPF
Supt. New Jersey State Police, Trenton, N. J.

As a result of this kidnapping, the U.S. Congress passed a bill called the Lindbergh Law. The law made it a federal crime to take a kidnap victim across a state line or to use the postal service to send a ransom demand. This law allowed the FBI and other federal agencies to become involved in solving kidnappings and rescuing people who had been taken.

The Lindberg's Information Wanted Poster.

WORLD WAR II

Charles Lindbergh was impressed with the advances Germany was making in aircraft design and technology in the 1930s. He became convinced that, if there were a war, the German air force would defeat the forces of any country that fought against Germany.

Planes from the USS Essex aircraft carrier dropping bombs on Hokadate, Japan, July 1945. World War 2, Pacific Ocean.

In 1938, Germany, under the Nazi government of Adolf Hitler, gave Lindbergh a German medal of honor. This upset many in the United States, who felt Lindbergh was giving support to a terrible government that was already carrying out horrible actions in its own country and preparing for war with other countries.

Famed aviator Charles A. Lindbergh with
Maj. Thomas B. McGuire

World War II began in 1939, and Germany swiftly conquered much of Europe. There was pressure for the United States to enter the war on the side of Great Britain and the occupied countries like France and the Netherlands. Lindbergh

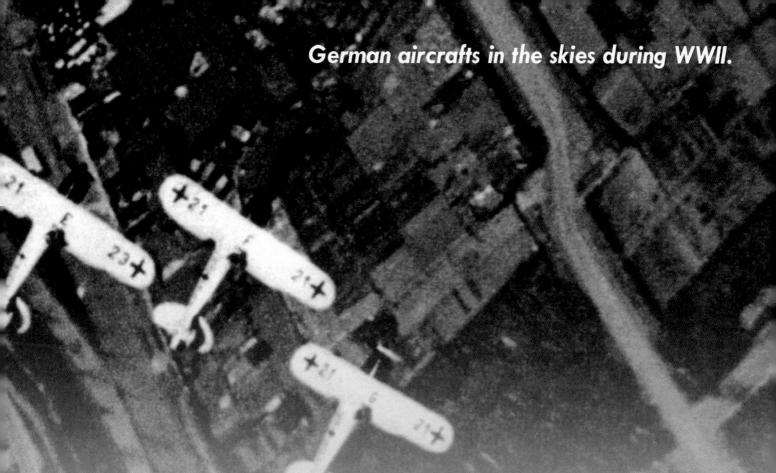

German aircrafts in the skies during WWII.

spoke out against the U.S. joining the war. He criticized the U.S. government and, when President Roosevelt responded negatively, Lindbergh resigned his commission in the military. Some people accused Lindbergh of working for the Germans.

Al Williams, Charles Lindbergh and Jimmy Doolittle

After Japan, an ally of Germany, attacked the United States in 1941, Lindbergh dropped his opposition to the U.S. entering the war. He tried to re-join the air force, but was turned down. He went to work as a test pilot for companies developing new warplanes for the military effort. He also developed new techniques that let the U.S. planes fly further before having to refuel.

In 1944, Lindbergh went to the Pacific as a military adviser. He was a civilian, but he still managed to fly more than fifty combat missions against Japanese targets.

Charles Lindbergh and his wife visiting Japan.

Charles Lindberg and Anne Morrow Lindberg

LATER YEARS

After World War II, Charles Lindbergh tried to live quietly, without attracting much attention. He worked as a consultant with the air force, and in 1954 President Eisenhower gave him back his military commission and promoted him to the rank of general.

Working with the Boeing Aircraft company and Pan American World Airways, Lindbergh also helped in the development of commercial jet aircraft, and with the design of the Boeing 747 passenger jet.

In 1953, Lindbergh published a book about his flight across the Atlantic, The Spirit of St. Louis. The book sold well, and Lindbergh won a great literary award, the Pulitzer Prize, for it.

Charles Lindbergh died at the age of 72, of cancer, at his home in Hawaii.

The grave and marker of Charles Lindbergh on his Hawaiian home island of Maui.

ONE PERSON CAN MAKE A DIFFERENCE

A person with vision and determination can do great things in this world. For other examples, read the Baby Professor books *A Rich Man In Poor Clothes: The Story of St. Francis of Assisi* and *The Legends of Sports: Tiger Woods, Michael Jordan and Muhammad Ali.*

Erik Lindbergh, grandson of famed aviator Charles Lindbergh, unveils a plaque commemorating his grandfather to dedicate the 747 Clipper Lindbergh, a NASA airborne infrared observatory known as SOFIA.

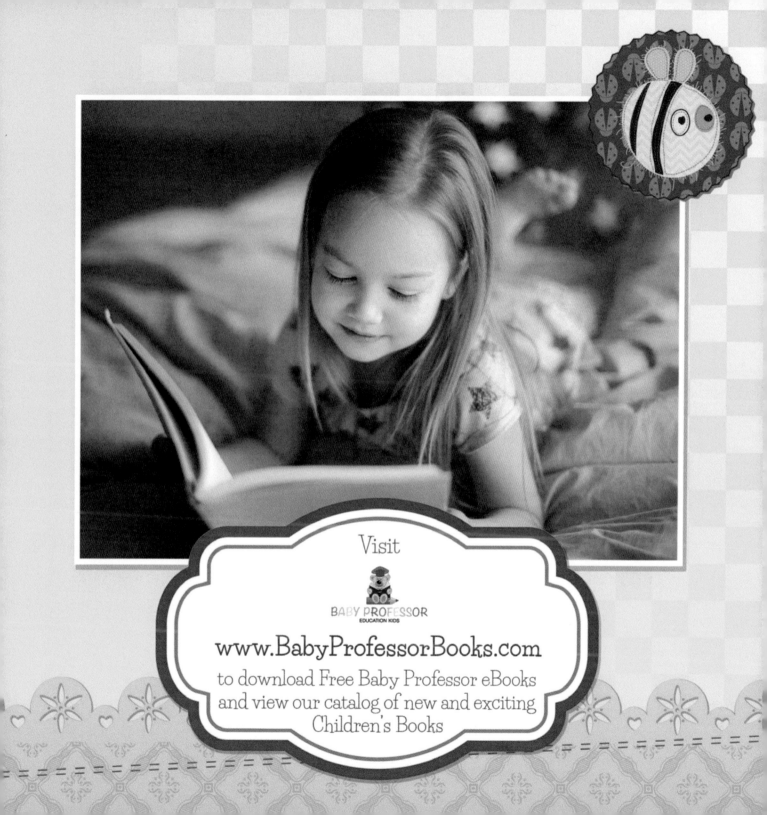

Made in the USA
Las Vegas, NV
06 March 2022

45127515R00040